What Are STARS?

I LIKE SPACE!

Carmen Bredeson

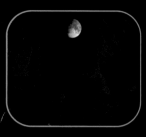

astronomer (uh STRAH noh mur)
A scientist who studies things in space.

constellation
(con stuh LAY shun)
Groups of stars in which people think they see the shapes of people and animals.

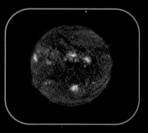

dwarf (dworf)
Smaller than others of the same kind.

energy (EH nur jee)
Light and heat.

galaxy (GA lek see)
A very large group of stars.

CONTENTS

How is a star made?

A star is born when gas and dust in space make a giant ball. The ball spins tighter and tighter. It gets very hot inside. The gas gets so hot that it turns into energy that we can see.

hot, young, blue stars

How long do stars shine?

Giant stars use their gas fast. They shine for millions of years. Medium-sized stars use their energy more slowly. They shine for billions of years. Small stars take an even longer time to run out of energy.

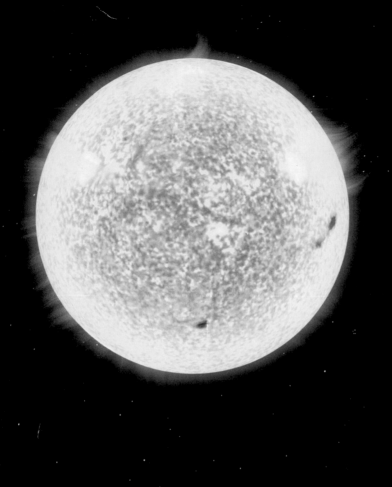

Fun Fact

Some stars are twins or triplets.
They were born at the same time
from the same gas cloud.

What happens when a star gets old?

When big stars run low on gas, they puff up into red supergiants. Then they blow up.

This star is turning into a white dwarf star.

A medium or small star slowly cools off. It shrinks into a white dwarf. It still shines, but it is much smaller.

Fun Fact

When a red supergiant blows up, sometimes it turns into a black hole. Nothing can get out of a black hole—not even light!

Is the Sun a star?

Yes, the Sun is a medium-sized star.
It looks bigger than other stars
because it is closer to Earth.
The Sun is the only star we see
during the day.

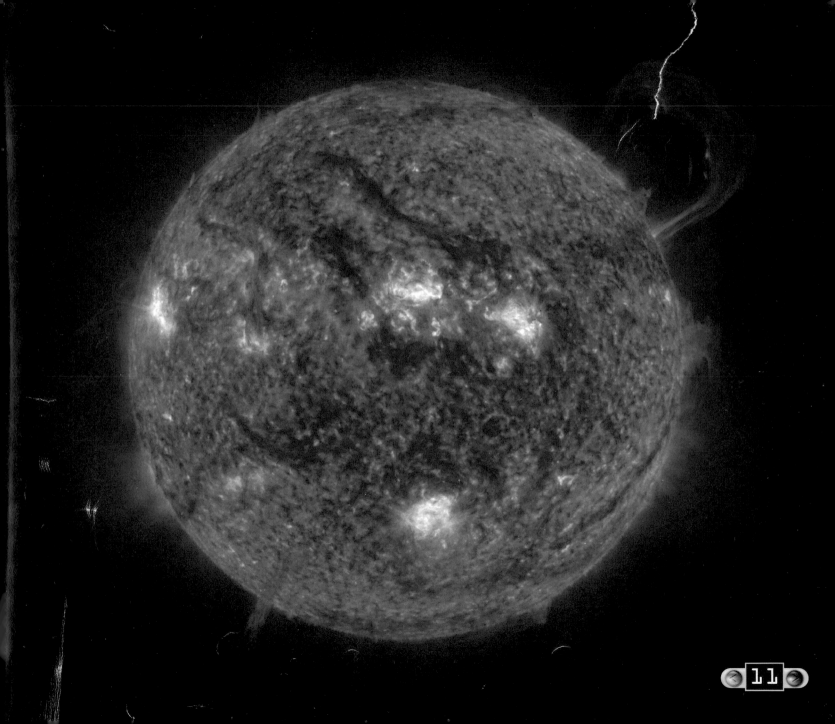

Why are stars different colors?

The color of a star tells how hot it is.

Our Sun is yellow.

Yellow stars are medium-hot.

Red stars are cooler than the Sun.

Blue or white stars are the biggest
and hottest stars.

Red Dwarf

Our Sun

Blue-white Supergiant

Red Giant

What are shooting stars?

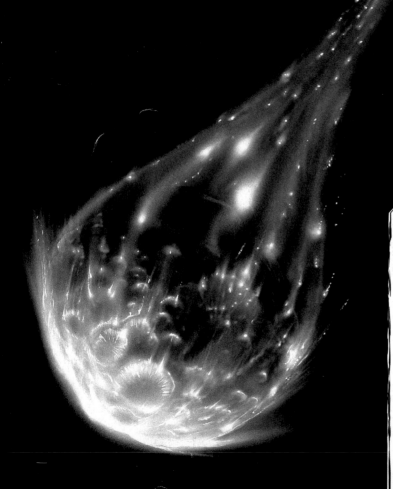

Shooting stars are not stars at all. They are rocks from space. When the rocks zip through Earth's air, they start to burn. The burning rocks make streaks of light in the sky.

shooting stars

15

Do stars have planets?

The Sun has eight planets. One of them is Earth. The planets go around the Sun. Astronomers have found planets around other stars too. Nobody knows if there are living things on other planets.

Why do stars twinkle?

The stars themselves do not really twinkle, but it looks like they do. Light from the stars passes through the air around Earth. The air makes the starlight move a little, or twinkle.

Fun Fact

All stars are round. They are not shaped like stars with points.

How long does starlight take to reach Earth?

Light from the Sun takes eight minutes to reach Earth. Proxima Centauri (PRAHK see muh sen TOR ee) is the next closest star. It takes light from this star four *years* to reach Earth. We see this star as it looked four years ago.

What is a constellation?

Long ago, people looked at the night sky. They connected the dots of the stars into shapes. They named some of the shapes after animals and other things. The shapes are called constellations.

This star chart was made about 500 years ago.
Orion the Hunter is one constellation.

How many constellations are there?

Gemini

Auriga

Capella

Betelguese

Perseus

Aldeberan

Orion

Taurus

Rigel

People on Earth have named 88 constellations. Some are named for objects and animals. Others are named for monsters and people from stories of long ago.

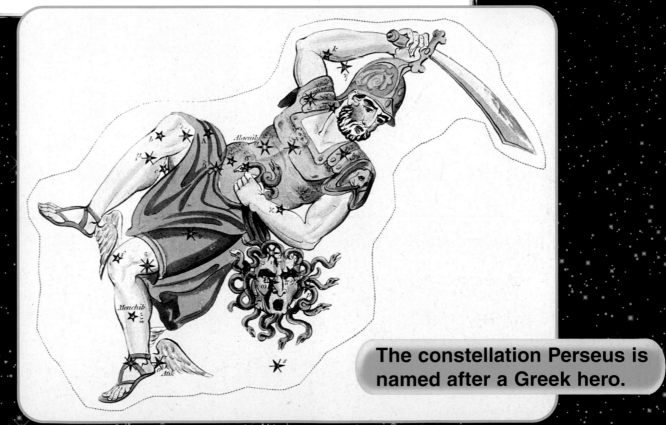

The constellation Perseus is named after a Greek hero.

Where do stars go during the day?

Stars do not go anywhere. You just cannot see them when the Sun is shining. At night, the Sun shines on the other side of Earth. The sky on your side is now dark, so you can see the stars again.

You can see the Big Dipper at night.
It is part of the Great Bear constellation.

Is it safe to look at stars?

This is how some stars look in a telescope.

You should never look at the Sun.

It could hurt your eyes or make you blind.

The other stars are far, far away.

You can safely look at them with your eyes,

binoculars, or a telescope.

The Andromeda galaxy looks like a star from Earth. But a telescope shows it is made of billions of stars.

Who studies stars?

Astronomers (a STRAH nuh murz) study the sky to learn about stars.

Engineers build telescopes that help us learn about stars.

Planetarium (pla nih TAIR ree uhm) workers show people how the night sky looks.

Teachers help students learn about stars and space.

Books

Mitton, Jacqueline. *Once Upon a Starry Night: A Book of Constellations.* London: Frances Lincoln, 2005.

Sasaki, Chris. *Constellations: A Glow-in-the-Dark Guide to the Night Sky.* New York: Sterling Publishing Co. Inc., 2006.

Simon, Seymour. *Destination Space.* New York: Harper Collins Publishers, 2002.

Web Sites

Astronomy for Kids.

http://www.kidsastronomy.com/stars.htm

NASA. Space Place.

http://spaceplace.nasa.gov/en/kids

Enchanted Learning: Zoom Astronomy

http://www.enchantedlearning.com/subjects/astronomy/

INDEX

To Kate, our shining star

Enslow Elementary, an imprint of Enslow Publishers, Inc.

Enslow Elementary® is a registered trademark of Enslow Publishers, Inc.

Library of Congress Cataloging-in-Publication Data

Bredeson, Carmen.
  What are stars? / Carmen Bredeson.
    p. cm. — (I like space!)
  Summary: "Introduces early readers to subjects about space in Q&A
    format"—Provided by publisher.
  Includes bibliographical references and index.
  ISBN-13: 978-0-7660-2943-9
  ISBN-10: 0-7660-2943-3
  1. Stars—Juvenile literature. I. Title.
  QB801.7.B755 2008
  523.8–dc22

2007002912

Printed in the United States of America

10 9 8 7 6 5 4 3 2 1

Every effort has been made to locate all copyright holders of material used in this book. If any
errors or omissions have occurred, corrections will be made in future editions of this book.

To Our Readers: We have done our best to make sure all Internet Addresses in this book were
active and appropriate when we went to press. However, the author and the publisher have
no control over and assume no liability for the material available on those Internet sites or on
other Web sites they may link to. Any comments or suggestions can be sent by e-mail to
comments@enslow.com or to the address on the back cover.

Cover Photograph: NASA/ESA/Hubble Heritage Team (STScI/AURA)

Illustration Credits: Carl M. Feryok (astronauts); © 2007 by Stephen Rountree
(www.rountreegraphics.com), pp. 6–7, 18–19.

Photo Credits: Atlas Photo Bank/Photo Researchers, Inc., p. 14; Courtesy NASA/JPL-
Caltech, pp. 16–17; Eurelios/Photo Researchers, Inc., p. 15; Gerard Lodriguss/Photo
Researchers, Inc., pp. 24, 27; © istockphoto/Rob Sylvan, p. 2 (astronomer); © 2007 Jupiter
images Corporation, pp. 2 (constellation), 20–21, 25; NASA/ESA/A. Feild (STScI), p. 13;
NASA/ESA/Hubble Heritage Team (STScI/AURA), pp. 5, 8; NASA Jet Propulsion
Laboratory (NASA-JPL), p. 9; Sheila Terry/Photo Researchers, Inc., p. 23; Shutterstock,
blue starfield background and pp. 28, 29; SOHO (ESA/NASA), pp. 2 (sun), 11.

Series Literacy Consultant:
Allan A. De Fina, Ph.D.
Past President of the New Jersey Reading Association
Chairperson, Department of Literacy Education
New Jersey City University, Jersey City, New Jersey

Series Science Consultant:
Marianne J. Dyson
Former NASA Flight Controller
Science Writer
www.mdyson.com

Enslow Elementary
an imprint of
Enslow Publishers, Inc.
40 Industrial Road
Box 398
Berkeley Heights, NJ 07922
USA
http://www.enslow.com